TECHNOLOGIES
AND
STRATEGIES
IN BATTLE

THE BATTLE OF
HASTINGS

Russell Roberts

Mitchell Lane
PUBLISHERS

P.O. Box 196
Hockessin, Delaware 19707
Visit us on the web: www.mitchelllane.com
Comments? email us: mitchelllane@mitchelllane.com

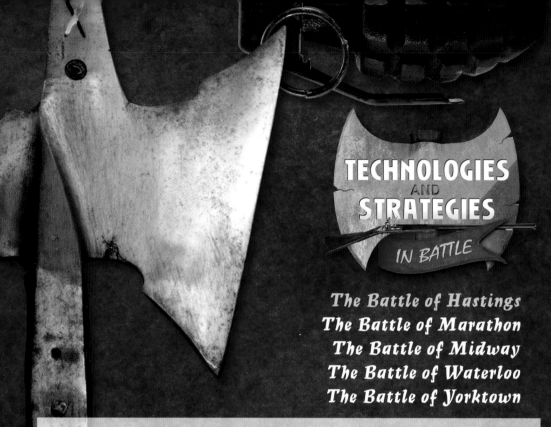

TECHNOLOGIES AND STRATEGIES IN BATTLE

The Battle of Hastings
The Battle of Marathon
The Battle of Midway
The Battle of Waterloo
The Battle of Yorktown

ABOUT THE AUTHOR: Russell Roberts has written and published nearly 40 books for adults and children on a variety of subjects, including baseball, memory power, business, New Jersey history, and travel. He has written numerous books for Mitchell Lane Publishers, including *The Life and Times of Nostradamus, Poseidon,* and *The Cyclopes.* He lives in Bordentown, New Jersey, with his family and a fat, fuzzy, and crafty calico cat named Rusti.

PUBLISHER'S NOTE: The facts on which the story in this book is based have been thoroughly researched. Documentation of such research can be found on page 45. While every possible effort has been made to ensure accuracy, the publisher will not assume liability for damages caused by inaccuracies in the data, and makes no warranty on the accuracy of the information contained herein.

To reflect current usage, we have chosen to use the secular era designations BCE ("before the common era") and CE ("of the common era") instead of the traditional designations BC ("before Christ") and AD (*anno Domini,* "in the year of the Lord").

Printing   1   2   3   4   5   6   7   8   9

Library of Congress Cataloging-in-Publication Data
Roberts, Russell, 1953–
 The Battle of Hastings / by Russell Roberts.
   p. cm. — (Technologies and strategies in battle)
 Includes bibliographical references and index.
 ISBN 978-1-61228-075-2 (library bound)
 1. Hastings, Battle of, England, 1066—Juvenile literature. I. Title.
 DA196.R63 2011
 942.02'1—dc22
                                          2011000605

eBook ISBN: 9781612281575

                                          PLB

CONTENTS

Chapter 1

Late in the afternoon on Sunday, October 14, 1066, King Harold Godwinson of England stood under a tree atop Senlac Hill, watching his army fight the Battle of Hastings. If his men could hold on until nightfall—just a little bit longer—victory would be his.

So far everything had gone well for Harold. Since early that morning, his army had successfully resisted the attacks of the invading Normans, led by Duke William of Normandy. The English soldiers were using the strategy of the shield wall. All the soldiers in the front raised their shields over their heads and held them close together. The kite-shaped shields were made of lime wood, a hardwood native to England, and measured about 36 inches by 15 inches (90 centimeters by 38 centimeters).[1] When arrows shot by enemy archers came hurtling through the air, they bounced off the raised shields and fell harmlessly to the ground. It was as if the soldiers were covered with a protective barrier. Although some arrows made it through the shield wall, the soldiers they hit were quickly replaced. Thanks in part to the shield wall, the English had

The Arrow That Changed History

managed to thwart attacks by the Normans all day.

The shield wall posed a particular problem for the Norman archers, but it was not the only one they faced in this battle. Normally the archers, once their supply of arrows was exhausted, would pick up the arrows fired by the enemy and shoot them back. However, the English had few, if any, archers at this battle. Thus there were no arrows lying around for the Norman archers to pick up. The effectiveness of the Norman archers—one of the strengths of the Norman army—had been greatly reduced.

Seeing his archers struggling, William sent the two other parts of his army—the infantry and cavalry—toward the English. However, these troops had also failed to break down the English shield wall.

Lined up along the crest of a ridge on Senlac Hill, the English occupied the high ground, with the Normans below them. The Normans had to attack by rushing up the hill—always a difficult thing to do, and something that offset their powerful cavalry.[2] The English had stood on the high ground and waited for them. As the Normans repeatedly attempted to climb the hill, the English threw spears, javelins, and even rocks and hammers down at them. In addition, the top English soldiers, known as housecarls, wielded the fearsome Danish battle-ax (see page 9), a vicious weapon that could split the skull of a charging horse with one blow. The Normans were driven back every time.

Harold looked around. The grass was red and slick with blood. Bodies of soldiers from both armies lay everywhere, many

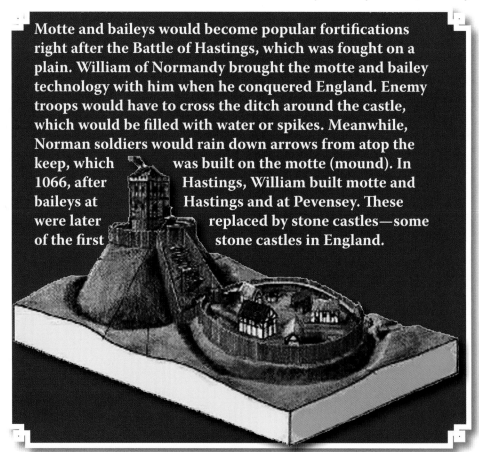

Motte and baileys would become popular fortifications right after the Battle of Hastings, which was fought on a plain. William of Normandy brought the motte and bailey technology with him when he conquered England. Enemy troops would have to cross the ditch around the castle, which would be filled with water or spikes. Meanwhile, Norman soldiers would rain down arrows from atop the keep, which was built on the motte (mound). In 1066, after Hastings, William built motte and baileys at Hastings and at Pevensey. These were later replaced by stone castles—some of the first stone castles in England.

mangled beyond recognition. Like many of his soldiers, Harold was tired. If the English could just hold on until nightfall, they could claim victory.

Harold saw the Norman archers approaching for another assault. He tightened his grip on his bloodstained battle-ax and waited.

William was trying something different. He commanded his archers to shoot their arrows not at the English soldiers in front with their shield wall, but rather high in the sky over them. The arrows would form a giant cloud that would rain down death on the soldiers behind the shield wall.

Now the Norman arrows did terrible damage. They flew in a high arc and then angled down to earth. Instead of hitting the protective shield wall in front, the arrows fell behind the shields, piercing the unprotected soldiers in the rear. They fell, grabbing at the arrows and screaming in pain.

Suddenly Harold cried out and dropped his battle-ax. He had been struck by an arrow in his right eye. The housecarls gazed at the king in horror as he grabbed the arrow and, with an agonized scream, pulled it out, broke it in half, and threw it down. Wracked with pain, he kneeled over his shield, blood pouring from the wound.[3] Word quickly spread among the English soldiers: The king was gravely injured. Their morale began to fade.

The Normans charged up the hill again. Swords clanged, spears flew, and battle-axes swung. The Normans were now making progress, punching through weak spots in the shield wall.

In agony, Harold was still trying to fight, but it was impossible to ignore his terrible wound—or the river of blood that flowed from it. He was having difficulty seeing. An arrow fired by an unknown Norman archer had changed everything.

Realizing that Harold was badly hurt, nearly two dozen Norman soldiers decided to finish him or die trying. They charged the weakened king. The housecarls guarding Harold saw the Normans coming and knew what they wanted.

The Bayeux Tapestry is an embroidered cloth that contains scenes from the Battle of Hastings. It clearly shows King Harold (far right) with an arrow in his eye.

Axes and swords tore through the air as the two sides slashed and cut at each other. Although many of the charging Normans were killed, others kept coming. Closer and closer they got to the king. The screams of wounded men rang out.

If Harold saw them coming, he would have known that they meant to kill him. There was nowhere for him to go.

The Normans got closer and closer. Would they get to Harold? Would the housecarls manage to protect him? The next few moments would determine England's future.

The Danish Battle-Ax

The primary weapon used by the housecarls at the Battle of Hastings was the Danish battle-ax. Known also as the Danish ax or even just the Dane ax, this very effective weapon inflicted massive injuries on soldiers and horses alike.

The Danish battle-ax was probably designed for agricultural use. Although it resembles an ax, instead of having a thick handle and a large, heavy head for cutting down trees or splitting logs, the Dane ax is lightweight, weighing only about 3 pounds (1.4 kilograms). It can easily be held in both hands and swung with plenty of force.

The Danish ax was approximately 3 feet 6 inches (about one meter) long and had an extremely sharp, thin, curved blade that provided a long cutting edge. Swung with both hands in an over-the-left-shoulder motion, it was designed to hit opponents on their unshielded side. Once hit by this fearsome weapon, a person or animal usually did not get back up. An image of a housecarl at Hastings shows him using a Danish ax to split open the head of a charging horse.

Among the famous historical figures who are believed to have used the Danish battle-ax is Richard the Lionheart, the iconic twelfth-century king of England.

Danish battle-ax

Chapter 2

Centuries ago, Normandy—the land of the Normans—was an independent country known as the Duchy of Normandy. It is now a region in northern France across the English Channel from Great Britain. Some people may recognize Normandy as the invasion site of the Allied forces in World War II.

The Normans were originally Vikings. (The word *Normandy* comes from other names for the Vikings: Northmen and Norsemen.[1]) During the eighth and ninth centuries, they frequently raided the coastlines of the kingdoms that would eventually become the country of France. In the year 911, in an effort to stop the Vikings from continually attacking these lands, Emperor Charles III (also known as Charles the Simple) gave them a large amount of land on which to live. In return he asked for their obedience.

Soon after these Vikings settled in the area, the two cultures—the Viking and the one that already existed in Normandy—began to mingle. However, the Normans never lost their warlike Viking characteristics. Before invading England they had already achieved military success in

The Armies and Their Weapons

areas that are part of modern Italy.

The Battle of Hastings took place during the Medieval Era, or Middle Ages, of European history (500 to 1500 CE). Warfare changed greatly over that thousand-year period.

The term *Medieval Era* often conjures up images of knights in shining armor on horseback. Although soldiers who fought at Hastings were armored, knights covered in plate armor came along years and years after the Battle of Hastings.

The main armor of the Norman soldier and the English housecarl was called a hauberk. This was a shirt of mail that usually reached down to the knees. It was made of interlocking metal rings that were woven into the fabric of the garment. It had a split in front and back so that the wearer could ride a horse. With

Even though a king ruled England, the country was divided into four regions—Northumbria, East Anglia, Mercia, and Wessex— each governed by an earl. The earls were very powerful. The king had to be careful not to anger the earls or he could face civil war.

its metal rings covering most of the body, the hauberk was designed for protection. Norman soldiers were pictured as wearing knee-length hauberks at Hastings. Hauberks were expensive, so common peasants and other occasional soldiers usually did not own them.

Another item of protection for the Normans and housecarls at Hastings was the helmet. Often called a "nasal helmet" because of a long metal piece that came down from the top and covered the nose, this helmet was made of iron or bronze formed to fit the head.[2]

Between the helmet and hauberk, the Normans and housecarls at Hastings were almost completely covered by armor of some type. The only exposed areas were the face, from about mid-

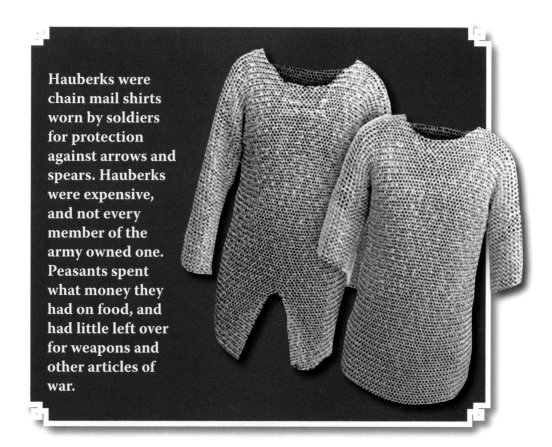

Hauberks were chain mail shirts worn by soldiers for protection against arrows and spears. Hauberks were expensive, and not every member of the army owned one. Peasants spent what money they had on food, and had little left over for weapons and other articles of war.

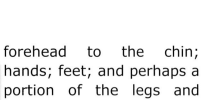
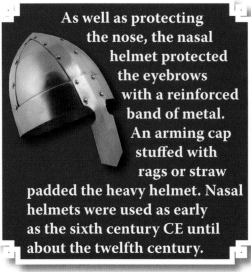

As well as protecting the nose, the nasal helmet protected the eyebrows with a reinforced band of metal. An arming cap stuffed with rags or straw padded the heavy helmet. Nasal helmets were used as early as the sixth century CE until about the twelfth century.

forehead to the chin; hands; feet; and perhaps a portion of the legs and arms.

A shield was another defensive tool. Today, shields are usually pictured as round, but the Norman shield was kite-shaped (as were the shields used by the English housecarls). It fit exactly in the space between a horse's neck and the rider's thigh, protecting the body of the rider; round shields did not provide the same protection.³

One of the primary weapons used at Hastings was the sword. Weighing about 3 pounds (1.4 kilograms) and roughly 40 inches (1 meter) long, the sword was double-edged, meaning that both razor-sharp sides could cut an opponent. It was more important that a sword have sharp edges than just a sharp point. The soldier used it in battle not to stab an opponent, but to slash and hack at him—the preferred method of attacking an enemy wearing a hauberk.

A main weapon for the Norman soldier was the lance. At the time of Hastings, the lance was about 10 feet (3 meters) long and made of a very hard wood, such as ash or applewood. It had a metal tip in

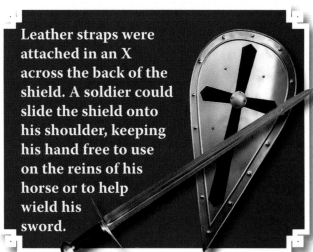

Leather straps were attached in an X across the back of the shield. A soldier could slide the shield onto his shoulder, keeping his hand free to use on the reins of his horse or to help wield his sword.

The cavalry was a critical part of the Norman army, and a major reason for their success in battle. However, the fearsome Danish battle-ax was a match for the Norman cavalry, because with one skillful blow an enemy could take down both a horse and rider.

the shape of a leaf. The pointed head of the leaf was meant to penetrate, while the sharp sides were designed to cut. Because the lance could break upon impact, most soldiers brought more than one to a battle. The soldier would attack, and if he was fortunate enough to survive, he went back to his army for another lance.

The sword and especially the lance were used by mounted soldiers known as cavalry. Throughout Europe, cavalry was replacing infantry as the most important part of an army, and

the Norman cavalry, which made up between 30 and 35 percent of its forces, was one of the key reasons they met with such success in battle. As writer Brian Todd Carey stated, "[Mounted] Norman knights became an irresistible juggernaut on the battlefield. By the middle of the eleventh century, the Normans were the pre-eminent heavy cavalry in western Europe."[4]

Naturally, a horse had to be very big and strong in order to carry a man with an armored shirt and several weapons. The Normans bred a special type of horse for the job, the destrier. "The careful breeding and management of . . . destriers was one of the secrets of Norman [military] success,"[5] wrote historian Timothy Baker. The destrier was a large, powerful horse with a strong back, legs, and hindquarters. It was trained to respond to the pressure from a rider's legs, since the rider needed both hands to carry his shield and weapons. Using the destrier, the Norman cavalry was feared throughout Europe.

Along with the horse and rider, there was one more important element: the stirrup. Used with a saddle that had a high pommel, the stirrup made horse and rider one unit by helping the rider keep his balance. When

The Normans used a specially bred warhorse called the destrier. Often referred to as a "Great Horse" because of its size, a destrier could be 15 or 16 hands high. (A hand is equal to approximately 4 inches, or 10 centimeters.)

charging, he could lean backward slightly while holding his lance in the crook of his arm. The result was a powerful blow with the full force of the charging horse and rider behind it.

Archers were another vital component of the Norman army. Typically unarmored, archers constituted around 15 percent of the Norman troops.[6] They used the self bow rather than the longbow (which came later, and is the bow we are most used to seeing in television shows and movies). Besides being shorter than the longbow, the string of the self bow was pulled back probably just to the chest, rather than to the ear. The arrows were effective for only 100 yards (90 meters).[7]

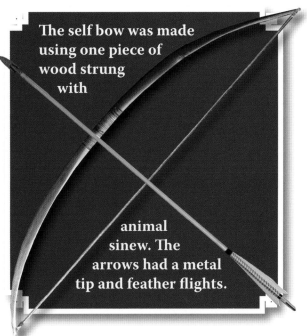
The self bow was made using one piece of wood strung with animal sinew. The arrows had a metal tip and feather flights.

The English army was called the fyrd, a concept developed several centuries before. The fyrd functioned much like a local militia; they were called out in times of emergencies. For every five hides of land (a hide was a land measurement of anywhere from 40 to 120 acres; a typical estate constituted five hides[8]), one soldier had to report to the fyrd to serve for a period of two months.

The fyrd was divided into the select fyrd and the general fyrd. The select fyrd were thanes (or thegns): warriors and peasants trained in warfare. The general fyrd (also called the Great Fyrd) were peasants, usually untrained and ill equipped. They could use anything from a spear to a hammer or rake in battle. They usually did not have armor, but dressed in a leather

Peasants who served in the English Army usually did not have uniforms or special armored clothes. Leather jerkins and inferior shields did not provide much protection during battle.

Jerkin

English shield

jerkin (sleeveless jacket) and a cap. When they had shields—which few did—they were anything from a piece of wood to a window shutter, with limited effectiveness.

The main component of the English army was the housecarls (also known as huscarls). Housecarls were professional soldiers; today we would call them mercenaries. These soldiers lived together, trained together, and made a superb fighting force with excellent military skills. Wearing armor similar to that of the Normans, their primary weapon was the Danish battle-ax. Being professional soldiers, housecarls took an oath to fight to the death for their lord. Harold had a force of housecarls at Hastings.

Unlike the Normans, the English forces used horses only for transportation, not for battle. They lacked the cavalry arm that the Normans used so well.

At Hastings the English also had few archers. The reason, ironically, had to do with one of the most resounding victories in English military history up to that point: the Battle of Stamford Bridge.

England in 1066

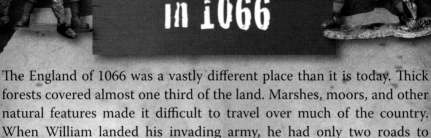

The England of 1066 was a vastly different place than it is today. Thick forests covered almost one third of the land. Marshes, moors, and other natural features made it difficult to travel over much of the country. When William landed his invading army, he had only two roads to choose from to get to London—England's major city—because forests and swamps prevented him from moving in any other direction.

The English people were divided into three classes: thanes (the highest), followed by ceorls (similar to the American middle class), and then slaves. However, these ranks were not set in stone. For example, it was possible for a thane to become a slave.

Sometimes owners freed their slaves. These slaves then became a new class, somewhere in a cloudy zone between ceorl and slave. Without the possessions or abilities of a ceorl to earn a living, but still higher in rank than a slave, these people could only pledge allegiance to a thane, who might give them some land or possessions in return for absolute obedience.

England's economy was based on agriculture, so most people were farmers. There were few towns as we know them today. People lived in homes built of wood (because wood was easily available; building with stone came later), usually by themselves. Sometimes several individual families would band together for protection. These groupings were the beginnings of towns and villages. The official religion of England at the time was Christianity.

Glastonbury Abbey

The most basic reason for the Battle of Hastings was to determine who would be the king of England. Harold Godwinson was crowned king upon the death of Edward the Confessor. William, the Duke of Normandy, believed he was the rightful king. The Battle of Hastings was fought to decide whether Harold or William would rule England. However, as is often the case in history, there is much more to the story.

The tale of the Battle of Hastings begins in the year 1002, when the English King Ethelred married Emma, the sister of King Richard of Normandy. Emma brought Norman ways and customs to England.

In 1013 the Danes invaded England. Fearing for the safety of her three children—Alfred, Edward, and Goodwife—Emma sent them to live in Normandy. When Edward returned from Normandy in 1042, he became king of England. Known as Edward the Confessor, he continued introducing Norman ways and customs into England. (He reportedly spoke the Norman language better than English.)

The Fight for Kingship

At this time in England the king was chosen by the witenagemot. This was a group of some of the richest and most powerful people in the country, such as bishops, earls, and the royal family.[1] Each of the four regions of England—Wessex, East Anglia, Mercia, and Northumbria—was controlled by an earl. The earl was responsible for keeping the peace, collecting taxes, and making certain that all aspects of his land were safe and the people were obedient to the king. In some ways the earl was similar to the governor of an American state.

Because of the earl's important role in English politics, he spent a lot of time at the king's royal court, where he was often involved in matters of national importance. The day-to-day operations of the earl's territory were left to the sheriff.

Wessex was the most populous and powerful of the country's regions, covering about one third of southern England. After the king, the Earl of Wessex was the most important man in the country. The Earl of Wessex at this time was Godwin (sometimes called Goodwin or even Goodwine). In 1053, his son Harold succeeded him as earl.

Edward the Confessor did not have any male heirs; that is, he did not have a son who would automatically become eligible to be named king after him. This opened the door for others to become king upon Edward's death.

On January 5, 1066, King Edward lay dying. As was the custom, many people were gathered around him, among them Harold. Just before he died, Edward reportedly stretched out his hand to Harold and said: "This woman [the queen] and all the kingdom I commend to your charge."[2] Shortly after that, he died.

Following Edward's death, the witenagemot assembled and named Harold the new king, as it seemed Edward had wanted. However, there was a problem. William, Duke of Normandy, had expected that he would become the new king upon Edward's death. Reportedly, Edward had told William years before that he would be his successor. If he had done so it would have made sense, for Edward was more Norman than English.

Born in 1027 or 1028 in Falaise, Normandy, William was the illegitimate son of Robert, Duke of Normandy. Almost nothing is known about his mother, except that her name was Herleva, and her father may have been a tanner named Fulbert.[3] Because of the circumstances surrounding his birth, he was sometimes called William the Bastard.

William felt that Harold had taken what was rightfully his—the throne of England. However, there was more to it than just Edward's supposed promise to William. Just two years earlier, Harold had met William in Normandy. The two had fought side by side, and William made Harold a knight. Harold swore an

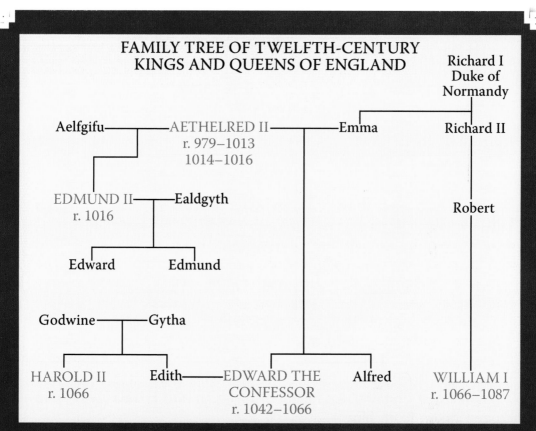

FAMILY TREE OF TWELFTH-CENTURY
KINGS AND QUEENS OF ENGLAND

Richard I
Duke of
Normandy

Aelfgifu—————AETHELRED II————Emma
r. 979–1013
1014–1016

Richard II

EDMUND II——Ealdgyth
r. 1016

Robert

Edward   Edmund

Godwine——Gytha

HAROLD II   Edith————EDWARD THE   Alfred   WILLIAM I
r. 1066   CONFESSOR   r. 1066–1087
                          r. 1042–1066

The path to becoming the king of England during this time was not very straightforward. This is why so many claimed that they should be the new king after the death of Edward the Confessor, and this is the reason the Battle of Hastings was fought.

oath of loyalty and service to William in the presence of important religious items, which gave the oath great importance.

The English considered this oath of much less significance than the Normans did. The English felt it was done under duress; Harold could not have refused to take the oath after being knighted, for it would have been a sign of disrespect to William. However, to the Normans, the oath was sacred; when Harold

took the crown as king of England, William and the Normans felt that he had betrayed his oath.

It had been known in Normandy that Edward was ill. When William received the news of the king's death, he was also told that Harold had assumed the throne. After hearing the news, William reportedly sat on a bench for a while, turning from one side to the other, undoubtedly a ball of emotions at the news of Harold's actions.[4]

William sent a formal protest to the English court, but he knew this would do little good. Harold had the crown, and the only way to get it from him was by force. William began planning to invade England.

From the moment he was crowned king, Harold knew that William of Normandy was not going to give up his claim to the throne without a fight. However, that wasn't Harold's only problem.

Harold's brother Tostig had once been the Earl of Northumbria, but he had been overthrown and banished to Flanders. Tostig felt that his brother had betrayed him, and that a grave injustice had been done to him. When Tostig heard that his brother was now king of England, he decided to return and reclaim what had been taken from him.

Realizing that he could not defeat Harold by himself, Tostig made an alliance with the Viking king of Norway, Harald Hardrada. (Hardrada also had a claim to the English throne.)

Harold anticipated that the main threat to him was going to come from William of Normandy. He kept the fyrd together throughout the summer in the south of England, waiting for an invasion from William that did not come. In fact, William had been preparing for an invasion, but it took a long time to gather the men, build the ships, and make other preparations. Finally, on September 8, 1066, with provisions running low, expenses mounting, and the fall crops ready to be harvested by the peasants who were part of his army, Harold could wait no longer. He ordered the fyrd to disband.

Shortly thereafter, the combined forces of Tostig and Hardrada, sailing 300 ships, landed in the north of England and began attacking Northumbria, sacking towns and devastating the countryside. Harold gathered his forces again and raced north with a speed unheard of in those times, covering more than 180 miles (290 kilometers) in a little over a week.

On the morning of September 25, Tostig, Hardrada, and two thirds of their army went to Stamford Bridge, where they expected to meet representatives from Northumbria and receive

Viking warships, called longships, had a fearsome reputation. Carrying a crew of about ninety, they could be powered by sail or by oar. They were at least six times longer than they were wide and had a shallow draft. They were therefore speedy and could sail in nearly any waterway. They could even be rowed right onto beaches. The natural lanolin in the woven wool sail kept the sail from getting   soaked.

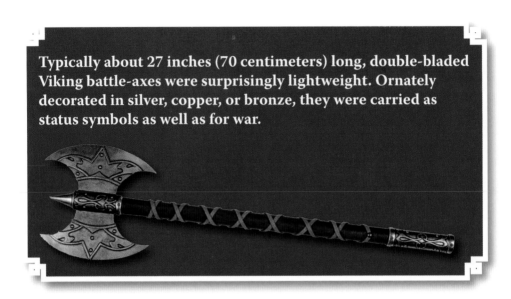

Typically about 27 inches (70 centimeters) long, double-bladed Viking battle-axes were surprisingly lightweight. Ornately decorated in silver, copper, or bronze, they were carried as status symbols as well as for war.

formal terms of surrender. Instead, what the invaders received, to their complete surprise, was Harold, who attacked them. When the Battle of Stamford Bridge was over, both Tostig and Hardrada were dead, and the Viking army was decimated. The survivors filled only 24 of the original 300 ships.

Harold had little time to savor his victory. On October 1, while he and his army were resting and recuperating at York—still in the north of England—word arrived that William of Normandy had landed his invasion force at Pevensey in the south. Harold's army was exhausted, both from their rapid march north and the Battle of Stamford Bridge. Even so, the king decided to travel south immediately—more than 250 miles (400 kilometers)—and meet this latest threat. By October 13, Harold had arrived at Caldbec Hill, 8 miles (13 kilometers) from Hastings, where the Normans were waiting.

The Last Viking Ruler

Harald Hardrada, the King of Norway, was one of the fiercest warriors of his time and a brutal ruler. His name—alternately spelled Hardraada—means "hard rule."

In a famous story about Harald that may or may not be true, he was attacking a city and laying siege to it but getting nowhere. He conceived the idea of pretending that he was dying, and he asked the priests in the city for help in arranging a Christian burial for him. Overjoyed that this violent man was finally going to become a Christian, the priests were only too glad to help. After he "died," they moved the coffin, with his body in it, into the city. All of a sudden Hardrada sat up, sending the priests running in all directions. He opened the gates, and his Vikings poured in and ransacked the city.

Hardrada was fatally pierced in the cheek and throat by an arrow at Stamford Bridge. His death is considered the end of the Viking era.

Harald Hardrada

Chapter 4

Before getting into details of the Battle of Hastings, there is a question that must be answered: Why did Harold fight at all that day? His army was depleted by the Battle of Stamford Bridge and worn out by rapid marching between the south and the north—hundreds of miles all together. There were so few housecarls and thanes—the best English soldiers—that they could be used only in small defensive groups and not for offense. Although they did not use horses in battle, Harold, the house-carls, and the thanes used them for travel. The foot-soldier archers could not keep up with their rapid pace and had been left behind. These stragglers continued to arrive during the battle.

So why did Harold fight?

One reason could be that he wanted to stop the Normans from raiding the surrounding countryside. As king, he was responsible for the welfare of the people. Another reason could be that, having arrived where the Normans were, Harold was impatient to fight; it was something he knew had been coming for a long time, and he wanted to get started.

The Battle

The most likely possibility is that Harold planned to take William by surprise, much as he had done with Harald at Stamford Bridge.[1] However, Harold arrived too late in the day for that; spies undoubtedly reported his arrival to William. It is very possible that when his troops came out of the woods on Caldbec Hill on the morning of October 14, they were surprised to see the Normans gathering not too far away. Harold had to figure out a different strategy.

Probably because Harold knew that his tired and depleted army could not successfully attack the powerful Normans, he decided to fight a defensive battle. He deployed his troops along the ridge of nearby Senlac Hill, blocking the road that led north to London. His army, adept with the shield wall, was

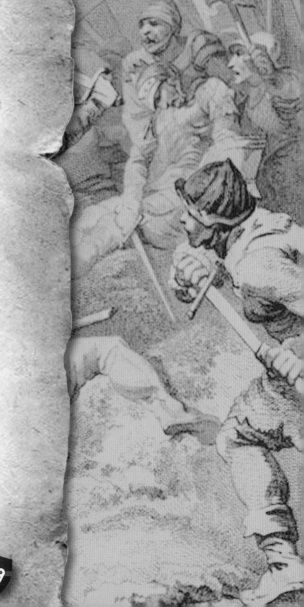

well suited for defense. Harold deployed his 8,000 men (2,000 housecarls, 6,000 fyrd) in ranks seven deep across a front about 800 to 1,000 yards (245 to 305 meters) wide. In the front, he placed his best men—the housecarls and the thanes. Behind them he placed the select fyrd. The untrained general fyrd took up the rear, behind the shield wall. (Estimates of the number of soldiers on each side vary. However, they all show that both sides had around the same amount.)

Harold set himself up, surrounded by housecarls, at the highest location, underneath an apple tree. His soldiers were approximately 50 yards (15 meters) in front of him, but because he was on higher ground, he could see everything from his position.

The Norman army was composed of three main divisions of troops: the Flemish, with William FitzOsbern, a Norman, at their head; the Bretons, commanded by Alan IV Fergant, the Count of Brittany; and the Normans, led by Duke William.

As both sides waited for the battle to begin, a single horseman—a minstrel named Taillefer—galloped out of the Norman ranks and charged the English. He wanted to spark the enthusiasm of the Norman troops by rushing forth, twirling his lance around, and then returning safely to his lines before the English could react. Unfortunately, instead of turning around, Taillefer's horse continued charging—right into a mass of English soldiers. Neither Taillefer nor his horse returned.[2] The Battle of Hastings had begun.

The Norman archers approached the English lines and shot wave after wave of arrows at them in an attempt to thin their ranks. Thanks to the shield wall, most of the arrows bounced away harmlessly. The archers, who were not trained in hand-to-hand fighting, withdrew.

Next, William tried an attack of his infantry. Holding the high ground, the English threw down on the Normans every type of projectile at their disposal—even rocks. It was difficult for the

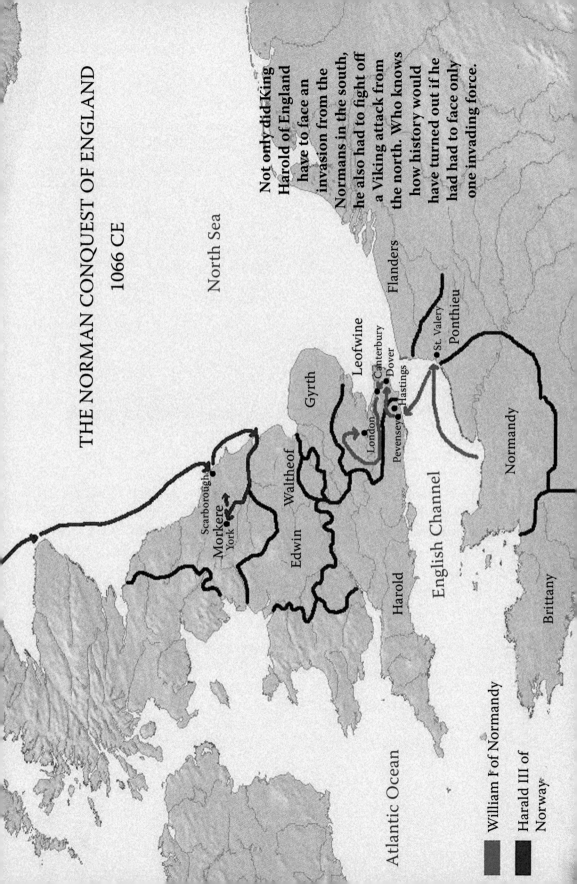

THE NORMAN CONQUEST OF ENGLAND
1066 CE

North Sea

Not only did King Harold of England have to face an invasion from the Normans in the south, he also had to fight off a Viking attack from the north. Who knows how history would have turned out if he had had to face only one invading force.

Flanders

Leofwine

Canterbury

Dover

Gyrth

Hastings

Scarborough

Waltheof

London

Pevensey

St. Valery

Ponthieu

Morkere

York

Edwin

Harold

Normandy

English Channel

Atlantic Ocean

Brittany

William I of Normandy

Harald III of Norway

About one hundred years after the Battle of Hastings, flags and banners displaying specific colors and symbols, known as heraldry, were used to identify who was who in battle. During the Norman conquest, it was not always easy to know the identity of someone whose features were hidden by armor.

Normans to charge uphill against this barrage of missiles. The English held.

From his command post, William could see that his attacks had failed. He called upon his cavalry to turn things around. The horses strained and panted as they climbed with the heavily armored humans on their backs. The men swung their swords and lances.

At this point the fearsome Danish battle-axes of the English came into full use. Many a Norman fell with his mount, never to rise again.

The English had steadily beaten back every attack of the Normans. On the left side, the discouraged invaders began retreating. Suddenly a rumor began circulating among the Normans: Duke William was dead! A slow retreat turned into mass confusion as word of his death spread like wildfire.

If William had been killed, would the Norman invasion collapse?

The Bayeux Tapestry

Tapestries are pieces of cloth with designs woven into them. The Bayeux Tapestry is not really a tapestry, because the designs are embroidered, or placed on top of the cloth. It is over 220 feet (68 meters) long, with pictures and text in Latin that show the events of the Norman Conquest of England, including the Battle of Hastings. It is housed in a museum in Bayeux, Normandy.

The origin of the tapestry is shrouded in mystery. The first known mention of it was in 1476, when it was discovered in the Bayeux Cathedral. However, it is almost certainly older than that. Many historians think that Duke William's half brother Bishop Odo ordered it made. Since Odo built Bayeux Cathedral, it is possible that he wanted the tapestry for the building's dedication in 1077.

There are numerous other theories about the tapestry's origin. One of the most sensational is that it contains coded messages aimed at disrupting the Norman rule of England.

Besides the questions surrounding its origins, the tapestry contains other mysteries. One is that several panels are missing, and it is unknown what images were on them. Popular guesses center around William's coronation as the king of England. The tapestry also contains some figures and images that historians cannot decipher, even to this day.

The tapestry chronicles not only the battle, but also the technology of the time. For example, the soldiers carry unadorned shields. It wasn't until about one hundred years later (1151) that coats of arms were used to identify military alliances.

Tapestry of Edward the King in his palace addressing Harold

When word that Duke William was dead swept through the ranks, the Norman retreat threatened to become a rout. At this critical juncture, Harold saw some of his troops disregard his instructions to stay put. They hurried down the hill after the fleeing Normans. Without their shield wall, command of the high ground, and protection of their fellows, the English troops were vulnerable. Realizing their predicament, Harold sent a group of housecarls commanded by his brothers Gyrth and Leofwine to bring these troops back.

It was too late. William—who was very much alive—pulled off his helmet and cried: "Look at me! I am alive, and will be the victor, with God's help!"[1] The Normans stopped running. Then, either led by William or at William's order, they charged the English who had foolishly left their comrades.

The two sides met in a fearsome clash of arms. Those with swords and battle-axes swung them fiercely. Others fought with whatever they had at hand. William's horse was killed from under him. But the English were no match for the Norman cavalry. All the English

The King Is Dead

in the pursuing group, including the king's brothers, were killed.

The Normans attacked again, and again—although their forces were depleted—the English held. Then, just as the Normans were retreating, the English soldiers in the center of their position decided to break ranks, as the others had done before, and clamber down the hill. They were wiped out just as the others had been.

Why did the English soldiers break ranks, especially after seeing how their other comrades had failed? One possibility is that Harold ordered them to, thinking that his men could inflict some further losses on the fleeing Normans. Another is that the soldiers did it on their own in order to retrieve swords, lances, hammers, and other weapons that had been discarded.

However, the likely reason is that William, as a part of his battle strategy, had his soldiers pretend to retreat so that some of the English would follow them, as they had the first time. They would then be vulnerable to attacks by his cavalry. As writer Antonio Santosuosso said: "Twice the Saxons were tricked into following the Normans down the ridge after William's men [pretended to withdraw]. There is no reason to doubt that this would have happened."[2]

It is uncertain what actually happened. Some sources say that the Normans did this deliberately, while others say they did not. However, what is clear is that William had learned to use his troops—archers, infantry, and cavalry—in combination, and it was too much for the English, already weakened by a major battle and then a long, hard march. William ordered his units to carry out a coordinated attack, which proved to be quite effective in weakening the English army. As historian Carey wrote: "William's use of alternate shock and missile attacks caused casualties and demoralized a force that received both forms of attack passively."[3] In other words, without an infantry or a cavalry force to use against the Normans, Harold's only choice was to have his soldiers stand on the ridge and simply absorb each Norman attack, and it was weakening his army.

The momentum of the battle had shifted. What had seemed like a certain victory for the English slipped away. It was late in the afternoon. Desperately Harold tried to hang on until nightfall, when darkness would end the battle.

However, William knew the English were tiring. He ordered another attack, and this time he made a critical change. He told his archers: rather than shoot at the front lines of the English defense, make the arrows fall at the back of the English soldiers, where the peasants of the general fyrd were located. Many of those men did not have shields.

The Norman archers did as instructed, and the arrows that rained down on the men behind the shield wall had terrible effect. While the men at the back fell, the Norman cavalry and

Harold's forces were tired after the Battle of Stamford Bridge.

infantry attacked from the front. Too many English had been killed throughout the day for the shield wall to remain effective. The English line began to crumble.

At around four o'clock, Harold was struck in or near his right eye. The path of an arrow had changed world history.

Harold tried to fight on, but the loss of sight and the pain of his wound dulled his movements. All around him the Normans were closing in. There were just too few English left.

The group of twenty Norman knights rushed Harold. Surrounded by housecarls, the king was not easy to reach, and

The site of the Battle of Hastings today is a peaceful, green area. Historians and students of the battle often visit here to try to understand what happened. While much is understood, much more remains to be discovered.

most of the Normans fell. Four of them—identified as Hugh of Montfort, Walter Giffard, Eustace of Boulogne, and Ivo—survived.[4] As one, they attacked the king.

The first attacker rushed at Harold with his spear. Harold put up his shield, but the spear punched right through it and lodged in his chest. A sword whistled through the air, gashing Harold in the neck just below his helmet, sending blood gushing. He fell.

He was struggling to rise when a third attacker drove his spear deep into his body. The fourth blow, a sword stroke to Harold's leg, was unnecessary.[5] The king was dead.

Word of his death quickly spread among the remaining English soldiers. Some housecarls may have continued to fight, but many others simply slipped away through the forest beyond. William pursued as many of the retreating English as he could, but darkness soon fell, finally ending the slaughter.

There were several reasons why the English lost at Hastings: Harold's army was weak after the Battle of Stamford Bridge; his strategy of staying strictly in a defensive mode and never attacking was too much for the English army to absorb against the Normans; and his army lacked critical elements, including archers and a cavalry, to fight the Normans. However, the biggest reason that William won was his strategy of using his forces in combination. "William's success," said Santosuosso, "was based on the proper chemistry of all forces at his disposal."[6]

Despite all we know about the Battle of Hastings, much is uncertain. For instance, some historians say Normans used crossbows, others say they did not; some say that William used his troops in combinations all day long, others say that he did so only at the end. However, the result was clear: William, Duke of Normandy, had defeated King Harold. He became the first Norman king of England.

Hastings Castle ruins

After Hastings

William's victory over Harold at Hastings made him the most powerful man in England. William might have thought that with that status, the English authorities would proclaim him king. After the battle he went back to Hastings and waited for the English to come to him. However, after a few days passed with no contact with anyone, William realized that he still had to force the issue. He subdued other cities—Dover, Canterbury, and Winchester—but still no word came from London, England's largest city and the seat of its government.

London was in no mood to submit to William. After learning of Harold's death, the witenagemot met and elected as king fifteen-year-old Edgar Aetheling (the son of the deceased nephew of Edward the Confessor). Two English earls, Edwin and Morcar, pledged allegiance to him, as did a religious leader, Archbishop Stigand.

William moved to the south end of London Bridge, where he routed Edgar's troops. He then began destroying various sections of the city, intending to isolate London.

The English realized that the game was up. Everyone, including Edgar Aetheling, came to William and pledged their loyalty to him. On December 25, 1066, William was crowned the king of England. He became known as William the Conqueror.

William's conquest turned England into a country influenced by France and Europe, rather than by the Scandinavian countries, as it had been. This changed England's language and culture. It also set the stage for a rivalry between England and France that would have a significant impact on world history.

William's coronation

Chapter 1. The Arrow That Changed History

1. *The Norman Conquest*, compiled by the Battle and District Historical Society (New York: Charles Scribner's Sons, 1966), p. 92.
2. Antonio Santosuosso, *Barbarians, Marauders, and Infidels* (Boulder, Colorado: Westview Press, 2004), p. 162.
3. Denis Butler, *1066* (New York: G.P. Putnam's Sons, 1966), p. 248.

Chapter 2. The Armies and Their Weapons

1. Jack Lindsay, *The Normans and Their World* (New York: St. Martin's Press, 1974), p. 3.
2. Medieval Spell: Medieval Helmets of the Norman Period, http://www.medieval-spell.com/Medieval-Helmets.html
3. R. Edward Oakeshott, *The Archaeology of Weapons* (Minneola, New York: Dover Publications, Inc., 1996), p. 177.
4. Brian Todd Carey, *Warfare in the Medieval World* (South Yorkshire, England: Pen & Sword Books, Ltd., 2006), p. 68.
5. Timothy Baker, *The Normans* (New York: The Macmillan Company, 1966) p. 30.
6. Antonio Santosuosso, *Barbarians, Marauders, and Infidels* (Boulder, Colorado: Westview Press, 2004), p. 160.
7. *The Norman Conquest*, compiled by the Battle and District Historical Society (New York: Charles Scribner's Sons, 1966), p. 93.
8. Denis Butler, *1066* (New York: G.P. Putnam's Sons, 1966), p. 111.

Chapter 3. The Fight for Kingship

1. Denis Butler, *1066* (New York: G.P. Putnam's Sons, 1966), p. 3.
2. Ibid., p. 22.
3. David C. Douglas, *William the Conqueror* (Berkeley: University of California Press, 1964), p. 15.
4. Butler, p. 45.

Chapter 4. The Battle

1. Brian Todd Carey, *Warfare in the Medieval World* (South Yorkshire, England: Pen & Sword Books, Ltd., 2006), p. 75.
2. Denis Butler, *1066* (New York: G.P. Putnam's Sons, 1966), p. 239.

Chapter 5. The King Is Dead

1. Antonio Santosuosso, *Barbarians, Marauders, and Infidels* (Boulder, Colorado: Westview Press, 2004), p. 163.
2. Ibid.
3. Brian Todd Carey, *Warfare in the Medieval World* (South Yorkshire, England: Pen & Sword Books, Ltd., 2006), p. 76.
4. Denis Butler, *1066* (New York: G.P. Putnam's Sons, 1966), p. 249.
5. Ibid.
6. Santosuosso, p. 164.

(All dates 1066)

January	Edward the Confessor, king of England, dies and is replaced by Harold Godwinson.
January–February	Duke William of Normandy decides to invade England and claim the throne.
June	Harald Hardrada, king of Norway, and Tostig, exiled brother of Harold Godwinson, make an alliance to invade England.
June–September	King Harold keeps the fyrd together in the south of England, waiting for William of Normandy to invade.
September 8	Harold disbands the fyrd before William arrives.
mid-September	Harald Hardrada and Tostig land in the north of England and start ravaging the countryside.
September 15	Harold races north with his army to face Hardrada and Tostig.
September 25	Harold defeats Hardrada and Tostig in the Battle of Stamford Bridge.
September 28	Duke William of Normandy lands at Pevensey on the southern coast of England, beginning his invasion.
October 1	At York, celebrating his victory, Harold learns of William's invasion. He rushes south to face William.
October 14	The English troops line up on the ridge of Senlac Hill to face the assault of the Normans below, who have come from Hastings. The English, fighting a defensive battle, repel repeated attacks by the Normans. Harold is struck by an arrow in the right eye. The English line, weakened throughout the day, starts to crumble, allowing several Normans to kill Harold and bring victory to William.

c. 850   The Chinese invent gunpowder.

911   Charles defeats Viking leader Rollo, making Rollo his vassal and converting him to Christianity. Rollo receives Normandy and marries Gisela, the daughter of Charles.

1000   Northern European farmers begin using iron instead of wooden wheels.

1002   Leif Eriksson travels down the coast of North America. King Ethelred of England marries Emma of Normandy.

1013   The Danes, led by Sweyn I Forkbeard, conquer England.

1017   King Canute divides England into four earldoms.

1042   Edward the Confessor becomes king of England.

c.1045   In China, Bi Sheng invents movable type.

1052   Edward the Confessor founds Westminster Abbey in England.

1053   Harold Godwinson becomes earl of Wessex.

1054   Chinese astronomers detect the Crab Nebula, which was created by an explosion in the constellation Taurus.

1066   A bright comet, someday to be known as Halley's Comet, appears in the night sky.

1067   William the Conqueror rebuilds the Tower of London.

1068   The massive 200,000-volume library in Cairo, Egypt, is destroyed.

1077   The Bayeux Tapestry is completed.

1085   The Domesday Book (similar to a census) is completed in England.

1086   Shen Kua of China begins work on a magnetized compass.

1087   William the Conqueror dies.

1091   The Normans conquer Sicily.

1120   Welcher of Malvern uses degrees, minutes, and seconds to measure latitude and longitude.

c. 1127   In China, gunpowder is used in cannons.

Works Consulted

Baker, Timothy. *The Normans*. New York: The Macmillan Company, 1966.

Bridgeford, Andrew. *1066: The Hidden History in the Bayeux Tapestry*. New York: Walker & Company, 2005.

Butler, Denis. *1066*. New York: G. P. Putnam's Sons, 1966.

Carey, Brian Todd. *Warfare in the Medieval World*. South Yorkshire, England: Pen & Sword Books, Ltd., 2006.

Douglas, David C. *The Norman Achievement*. Berkeley: University of California Press, 1969.

————. *William the Conqueror*. Berkeley: University of California Press, 1964.

Koch, H. W. *Medieval Warfare*. London, England: Bison Books, 1978.

Lindsay, Jack. *The Normans and Their World*. New York: St. Martin's Press, 1974.

Matthew, D.J.A. *The Norman Conquest*. New York: Schocken Books, 1966.

The Norman Conquest. Compiled by the Battle and District Historical Society. New York: Charles Scribner's Sons, 1966.

Oakeshott, R. Edward. *The Archaeology of Weapons*. Minneola, New York: Dover Publications, Inc., 1996.

Santosuosso, Antonio. *Barbarians, Marauders, and Infidels*. Boulder, Colorado: Westview Press, 2004.

Further Reading

Books

Henty, G.A. *Wulf the Saxon: A Story of the Norman Conquest.* Minneola, New York: Dover Publications, 2010.

Kroll, Steven. *Barbarians!* New York: Dutton Children's Books, 2009.

Lassieur, Allison. *The Middle Ages.* Mankato, Minnesota: Capstone, 2010.

Martell, Hazel Mary. *Everyday Life in Viking Times.* Mankato, Minnesota: Sea-to-Sea, 2006.

Tilton, Rafael. *Rulers of the Middle Ages.* Detroit, Michigan: Lucent Books, 2005.

On the Internet

The Battle of Hastings, 1066
http://www.battle1066.com

The Battle of Hastings—Norman Conquest
http://www.britishbattles.com/norman-conquest/battle-hastings.htm

Camelot International: The Battle of Hastings
http://www.camelotintl.com/heritage/battles/hastings.html

The Domesday Book
http://www.domesdaybook.co.uk/index.html

Timeline of the Battle of Hastings
http://www.battle-of-hastings-1066.org.uk/timeline-battle-hastings.htm

The Viking Museum
http://www.thevikingmuseum.com

PHOTO CREDITS: Cover picture—Frank Wilkin; p. 1—Francois Hippolyte Debon; pp. 6, 8, 9, 10–11, 12, 13, 14, 15, 16, 18, 19, 25, 26, 27, 31, 33, 37—cc-by-sa; p. 23—Carly Peterson; pp. 38, 39—Barbara Marvis; p. 41—JupiterImages. Every effort has been made to locate all copyright holders of materials used in this book. Any errors or omissions will be corrected in future editions of the book.

aetheling (AH-theh-ling)—Also spelled *atheling,* the heir apparent of a royal family, such as a prince.

alliance (uh-LY-unts)—A partnership between nations.

cavalry (KAV-ul-ree)—A group of mounted soldiers.

ceorl (CHAY-or-ul)—An Anglo-Saxon freeman of the lowest rank.

decimate (DEH-sih-mayt)—To destroy or wipe out.

duress (dur-ES)—Stress caused by threats.

elite (ee-LEET)—The best.

embroidery (em-BROY-duh-ree)—A design or decoration sewn onto a piece of fabric.

exile (EK-zyl)—Forced separation from one's country.

feudal (FYOO-dul)—Having to do with lords and their serfs.

hauberk (HAH-berk)—A tunic of chain mail.

illegitimate (il-ih-JIH-tuh-mit)—Born out of wedlock; outside the law.

juggernaut (JUH-gur-not)—A massive force that crushes whatever is in its path.

pommel (PAH-mul)—On a saddle, the front portion or knob that sticks up.

ransack (RAN-sak)—To search thoroughly for things to plunder.

recuperate (ree-KOO-pur-ayt)—To regain health or strength.

rout (ROWT)—A disastrous defeat.

tapestry (TAA-pus-tree)—A piece of fabric whose woven colored threads produce a design.

witenagemot (WIH-tuh-nuh-guh-moht)—An Anglo-Saxon council that meets to advise the king.